OCT 25 2006

J 973.2 THO
Thornton, Jeremy,
The French and Indian War /
PowerKids Press,2003.
24 p. :ill. (chiefly col.), col. maps ;

D1250528

3 9112 09143736 6

FRANKLIN LAKES PUBLIC LIBRARY

470 DEKORTE DRIVE

FRANKLIN LAKES, NJ 07417

(201) 891-2224

OCT 23 2006

BUILDING AMERICA'S
DEMOCRACY ™

The French and Indian War

Jeremy Thornton

Franklin Lakes Public Library
470 DeKorte Drive
Franklin Lakes, New Jersey 07417

The Rosen Publishing Group's
PowerKids Press™
New York

For my daughter, Ainsley Sarah

Published in 2003 by The Rosen Publishing Group, Inc.
29 East 21st Street, New York, NY 10010

Copyright © 2003 by The Rosen Publishing Group, Inc.

All rights reserved. No part of this book may be reproduced in any form without permission in writing from the publisher, except by a reviewer.

First Edition

Editor: Joanne Randolph
Designers: Michael J. Caroleo, Mike Donnellan, Michael de Guzman, Colin Dizengoff

Photo Credits: Cover, back cover, Library of Congress, Prints and Photographs Division; pp. 4, 7, 8, 11 (inset) © CORBIS; p. 11 courtesy of Map Division, The New York Public Library, Astor, Lenox and Tilden Foundations; p. 12 © Bettmann/CORBIS; p. 15 © SuperStock; pp. 16, 20 © Prints George; p. 19 National Archives of Canada.

Thornton, Jeremy.
The French and Indian War / Jeremy Thornton.
    p. cm. — (Building America's democracy)
Includes bibliographical references and index.
 Summary: A short history of the French and Indian War, focusing on its role in the development of the United States as a nation.
  ISBN 0-8239-6275-X (lib. bdg.)
   1. United States—History—French and Indian War, 1755–1763—Juvenile literature. [1. United States—History—French and Indian War, 1755–1763.] I. Title.
   E199 .T48 2003
   973.2'6—dc21
                                                    2001006022

Manufactured in the United States of America

Contents

CARTE
DES POSSESSIONS
ANGLOISES & FRANÇOISES
DU CONTINENT DE
L'AMÉRIQUE SEPTENTRIONALE
1755.

The War Begins

In the mid-1700s, Britain and France each controlled large **territories** in North America. They established **colonies** and had many **settlers** living on this **continent**. However, the two countries disagreed about the ownership of the land, and this often led to **skirmishes**. When war broke out between Britain and France in Europe, the settlers started their own war for control of North America in 1754. France and Britain each sent soldiers to help the settlers, and the French and Indian War began. Many Indians sided with the French, who usually treated the Indians with respect. The French traded with the Indians. The British seemed more interested in taking the land. The British did have some Indian allies, though.

This 1755 map shows the land that the French (in green) and the British (in yellow) claimed, as well as the land that they both thought they owned (in pink).

George Washington and Fort Necessity

The first real battle of the French and Indian War was at Fort Necessity in Pennsylvania. George Washington, who was only 22 years old at the time, dreamed of being a great military commander. His friend Governor Robert Dinwiddie of Virginia put him in charge of 400 soldiers. On May 28, 1754, Washington attacked and **defeated** a small French **scouting party**. He then built a small fort, which he called Fort Necessity, and he waited for the rest of the French to come. On July 3, the French came with 900 soldiers and quickly captured the fort. Washington had to **surrender**, and he marched home in defeat. It was not a good start for the British.

George Washington, shown here in a 1760 painting, would go on to become a great military leader and the president of the new United States of America.

FRANKLIN LAKES PUBLIC LIBRARY

Fort Duquesne and the Death of General Edward Braddock

The British sent Major General Edward Braddock to lead their troops against the French. On July 9, 1755, he marched with an army of 3,000 soldiers to take Fort Duquesne in Pennsylvania. Indian scouts told the French of Braddock's plan. The French decided to **ambush** the British. Around 700 French and Indians were part of the ambush. At the first attack, the French commander was killed, and the Indians were frightened by the British **cannons**. Soon the French soldiers pulled together, and the Indians surrounded the British. The British were forced to **retreat**. The French and the Indians chased them. They killed Braddock and more than 1,000 British soldiers. This was an important victory for the French.

This picture shows General Edward Braddock lying wounded *(center)*. He had been shot through the arm and the lung, but did not die for several days.

The British Plan

Britain's plan early in the war was to attack four French posts. The attack on Fort Duquesne had failed. A planned attack on Fort Niagara, in New York, was given up, because the French had too many soldiers there. The British launched an attack on Acadia, in Nova Scotia, Canada. In 1755, the British drove 6,500 French **supporters** out of their homes and burned their villages. The fourth point of attack was Fort Crown Point on Lake Champlain, in New York. In 1759, William Johnson led an army toward Fort Crown Point. They were met at Lake George by a French army. A battle was fought, and each side lost more than 200 men. Johnson and his men had to retreat. The British plan was not working.

This map from the 1700s shows the forts along the Hudson River. The inset shows the plan of Fort Crown Point, called Fort St. Frédéric by the French.

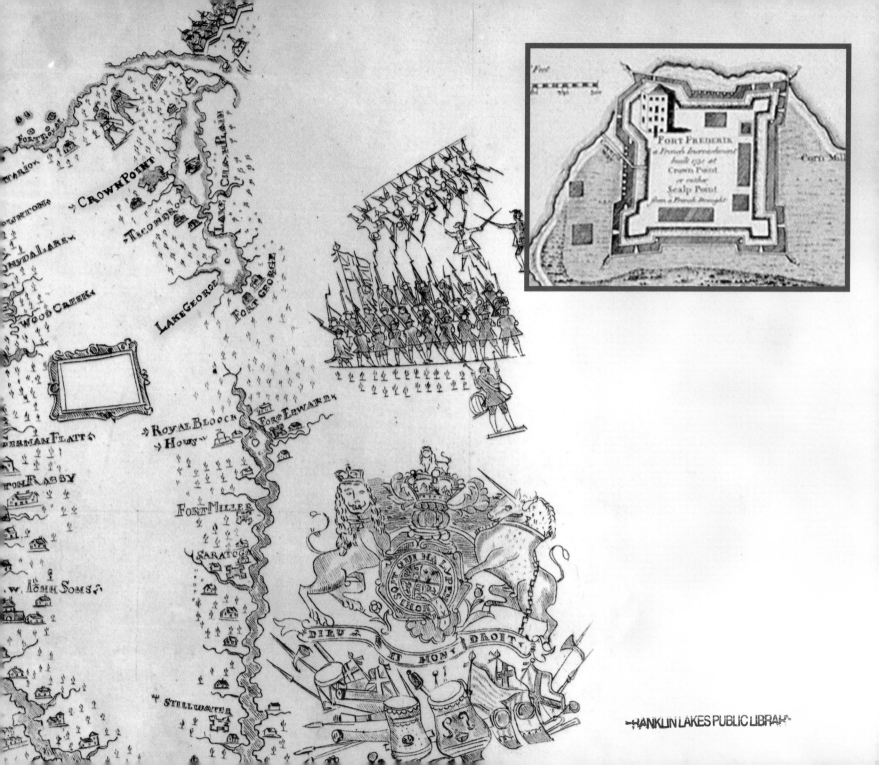

FORT ROYAL

TARBOX

CROWN POINT

TICONDROGE

ONYDA LAKE

LAKE CHAMPLAIN

WOOD CREEK

LAKE GEORGE

FORT GEORGE

DERMAN FLATTS

ROYAL BLOOCK
HOWS

FORT EDWARD

TON RABBY

FORT MILLER

W. IOHNSOMS

SARATOG

STILLWATER

FORT FREDERIK
a French Intrenchment
built 1731 at
Crown Point
or rather
Scalp Point
from a French Draught

Corn Mill

DIEU ET MON DROIT

HANKLIN LAKES PUBLIC LIBRARY

Enter Robert Rogers and His Rangers

The British did not do well in the early years of the war. They did not know how to fight well in the rough North American **terrain**. Robert Rogers was different. He had been born and raised in the **wilderness** of the American frontier. He had grown up with Indian groups. He joined the war in 1755 with a group of men, the **Rangers**. They knew the woods and were masters of ambush. They were an equal match for the French and the Indians. Lord George Augustus Viscount Howe, the new British commander, liked Rogers. He told Rogers to teach the British troops how to fight in North American terrain. Rogers taught the soldiers to hide and to wait for the enemy to get close before firing their guns.

Robert Rogers was born on November 18, 1731, in Methuen, Massachusetts. As a boy, he loved to explore the woods and the wilderness near his home.

Battle on Snowshoes

Robert Rogers wanted to spy on the French. In the winter of 1758, he and his men made **snowshoes**. Snowshoes let them walk on top of the snow. They hiked toward the French fort Ticonderoga in New York. On the way, scouts reported that some French were heading toward them across the ice. The scouts weren't quite right. The French were all around them. There was a **fierce** battle, and Rogers lost many men. Rogers's men fought bravely, though, and some were able to escape in the night. In Rogers's flight, he slid down a huge rock, now called Rogers' Rock, leaving his coat behind. The French found the coat and thought they had killed the famous Robert Rogers.

The Battle on Snowshoes, shown in this painting by Jean Leon Gerome Ferris, was a huge defeat for the British. Rogers was very upset at the loss.

FRANKLIN LAKES PUBLIC LIBRARY

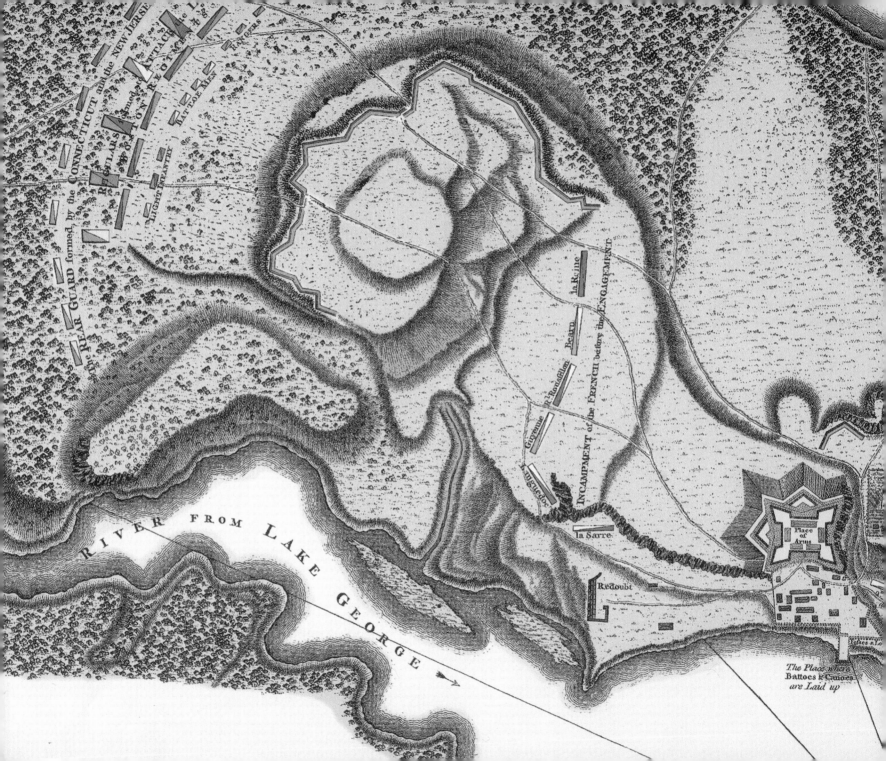

The REAR GUARD formed by the CONNECTICUT and the NEW JERSEY REGIMENTS covered by the REGULARS and the 55th REGIMENT

LIGHT INFANTRY

BATTEAU MEN

RANGERS

la Reine

Bearn

R. Rousillon

INCAMPMENT of the FRENCH before the ENGAGEMENT

Guyenne

Languedoc

la Sarre

Redoubt

RIVER FROM LAKE GEORGE

Place of Arms

The Place where Battoes & Canoes are Laid up

Lord Abercromby and the Attack on Fort Ticonderoga

In 1758, Lord Howe decided to attack Fort Ticonderoga. However, the French were ready for them. They were led by a talented general, the Marquis de Montcalm. At the first attack, Lord Howe was killed. Lord James Abercromby, the second in command, did not know what to do. He wasted valuable time. While Abercromby tried to decide what to do, the French had spent a day and a half preparing and building a wall. Finally he decided to attack again, even though the French had more men. The French hid behind the wall and shot at the British. The British tried six times to get past the wall, and each time they had to turn back. The British retreated. They lost 2,000 men because of Abercromby's failed plan.

The colored rectangles on this map show the positions of Abercromby's men as they attacked Fort Ticonderoga. It also shows where the French stood to defend the fort.

Jeffery Amherst and the Attack on Louisbourg

While Abercromby was getting crushed at Fort Ticonderoga, British generals Jeffery Amherst and James Wolfe were attacking Louisbourg. Louisbourg was a large French city in Nova Scotia, Canada, on the Atlantic Ocean. They sailed to Louisbourg with more than 12,000 men. They landed on the beach and fought off the French defenders. Upon reaching Louisbourg, they set up groups of cannons around the city. The British fired on the city night and day for more than a month, until the French finally surrendered. Encouraged by the victory, the British attacked Fort Duquesne again. The French decided to blow up their fort and to retreat. The tides of war were turning in favor of the British!

Louisbourg, pictured here, was a coastal city, an attractive target for the British. This is a view of the city near the lighthouse in 1758, when the British were attacking.

Louisburg in North America taken near the Light House when the city was besieg'd in 1758   Louisburg L'Amerique Sep. durant le dernier Siu

Drawn by Cap!. Ince of th   Engraved by P. Canot.

Attack on Quebec

Having won several important victories, the British turned their attention to capturing Canada in 1759. They set their sights on Quebec, the capital of New France. There they would meet Montcalm and the largest army France had in the Americas. Wolfe was the British general chosen to lead the **expedition**. The British arrived in Quebec, and for more than three months they **bombarded** the city. The repeated attacks had little effect. Finally the British soldiers climbed a small path up the side of a cliff and attacked the French on level ground. In the battle that followed, both Montcalm and Wolfe were killed. In the end, the French army was defeated. On September 13, 1759, the city of Quebec surrendered.

This battle plan from 1759 shows the attack on Quebec. Notice all the ships in the river. Wolfe and his men arrived on more than 150 ships to begin their attack.

British Victory

After the fall of Quebec, the British and the French fought several more battles. However, the French army had been crippled. The two countries signed the Treaty of Paris in 1763 to end the war. France gave up all of its land in North America to Britain except for Louisiana. Britain now controlled the 13 colonies in the northeast, Canada in the north, and the land as far west as the Mississippi River. Though the war with France was finished, the Indians were not done fighting the British and the settlers who remained on the land. The Indians continued to fight until the end of 1764. As a result of the French and Indian War, Britain became the **dominant** power in North America.

Glossary

ambush (AM-bush) To attack by surprise from a hiding place.

bombarded (bom-BARD-ed) To have attacked with artillery.

cannons (KA-nunz) Large guns with a smooth barrel.

colonies (KAH-luh-neez) New places where people move, who are still ruled by the old country's leaders.

continent (KON-tin-ent) One of seven large bodies of land on the globe.

defeated (dih-FEET-ed) To have won.

dominant (DAH-muh-nent) To be in control of another.

expedition (ek-spuh-DIH-shun) A trip for a special purpose, such as discovering new land or a scientific discovery.

fierce (FEERS) Very hard or violent.

Rangers (RAYN-jerz) A specific group of soldiers that fought for the English.

retreat (rih-TREET) To withdraw or to move back.

scouting party (SKOWT-ing PAR-tee) A group of people who are sent ahead to explore an area and then to report back to the leader.

settlers (SET-lurz) People who move to a new land to live.

skirmishes (SKER-mish-ez) Minor fights or contests between opposing parties.

snowshoes (SNOH-shooz) Shoes made for walking in the snow.

supporters (suh-POR-terz) People who help or fight for a group or a group's ideas.

surrender (suh-REN-der) To give up completely or to admit someone else won.

terrain (tuh-RAYN) The physical features of a piece of land.

territories (TER-uh-tor-ee) An area of land under the control of a government.

wilderness (WIL-der-nes) Wild land that has not been settled.

FRANKLIN LAKES PUBLIC LIBRARY

Index

Primary Sources

Cover: *The Death of General Wolfe,* painted by B. West, F.R.A.; engraved by H. B. Hall, from Library of Congress, Prints and Photographs Division. **Page 4:** This is a French map from 1755 that shows the French and English territories in North America. **Page 7:** James Peale painted this oil painting of George Washington around 1790. It was purchased by the city of Philadelphia, Pennsylvania, in 1849, and is now part of Independence National Historic Park. It is thought that the two men behind Washington to the left might be James Peale and his brother Charles Willson Peale. **Page 11:** From the Astor, Lenox and Tilden Foundation at the Map Division at the New York Public Library, this is an eighteenth-century map showing forts and towns along the Hudson River. At the top right is a depiction of a battle between the French and the British. At the bottom the shield says, in French, *Dieu et mon droit,* meaning "God is on my right." **Page 12:** This portrait of Robert Rogers is based on a 1776 engraving by Thomas Hart, published in London. Though not an authentic or accurate representation of Rogers, it is the best available. No known portraits of Rogers actually exist. This portrait is part of a series of engravings of American leaders, though Rogers was not an American (none of the colonists were at the time of the French and Indian War). **Page 15:** This painting by Jean Leon Gerome Ferris (1863–1930) is entitled *Battle of Rogers' Rock.* J. L. G. Ferris is known for his colonial revival paintings. **Page 16:** This map from 1758 was created for General Abercromby. The engraving is by an unknown artist. **Page 19:** This etching and engraving, hand-colored on laid paper, is entitled *A View of Louisburg [Louisbourg] in North America, Taken near the Light House When That City Was Besieged in 1758.* It was published on November 11, 1762, by Thomas Jefferys of London. The artist is Captain Charles Ince and the engraver is Pierre Canot. It is held by the National Archives of Canada. **Page 20:** *The First Large Scale Plan.* This is a correct plan of the battle fought on September 13, 1759. It was engraved in London by Thomas Jefferys in 1759.

Web Sites

Due to the changing nature of internet links, PowerKids Press has developed an online list of Web sites related to the subject of this book. This site is updated regularly. Please use this link to access the list.
www.powerkidslinks.com/bad/fiwar

FRANKLIN LAKES PUBLIC LIBRARY